# BONES

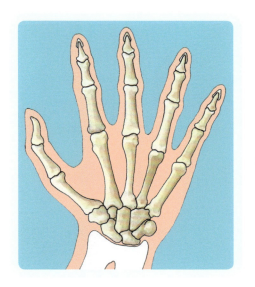

Written by Jonathan Emmett

Illustrated by Alan Baker

Photographs by Steve Lumb

## Collins

You have bones in your body.

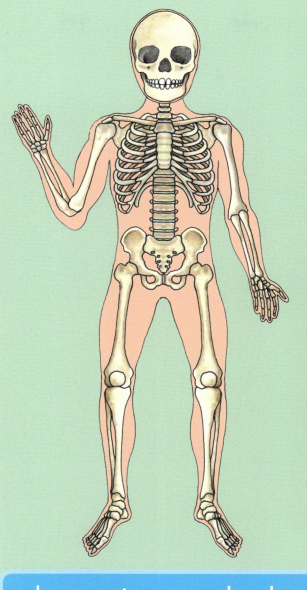

bones in your body

3

You have bones in your head.

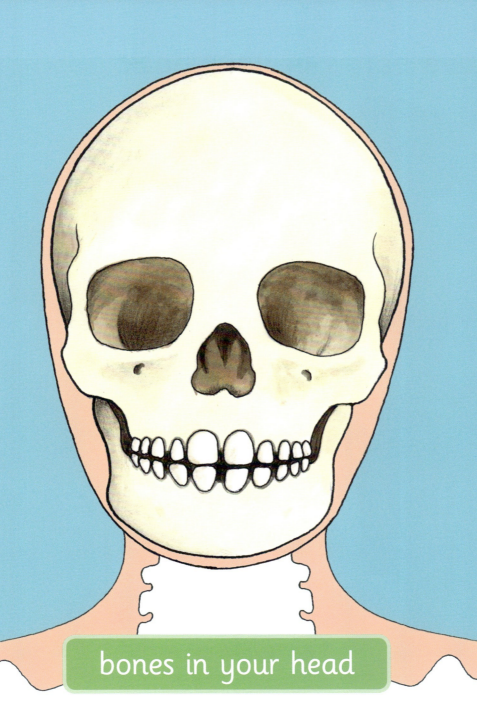

bones in your head

You have bones in your back.

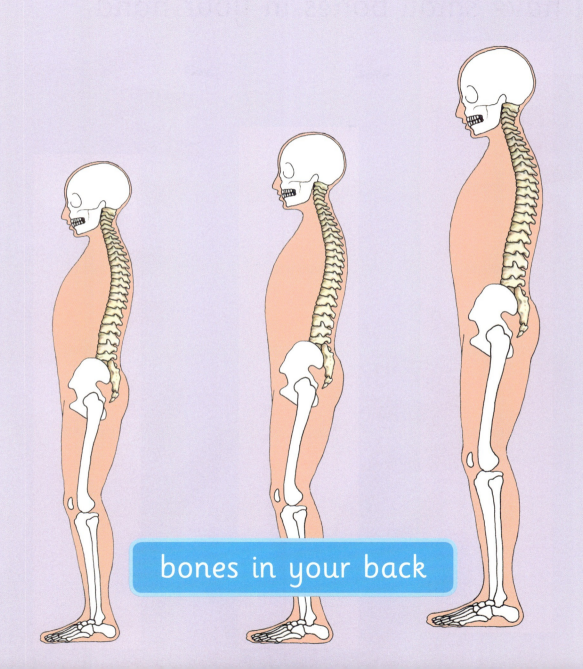

bones in your back

You have small bones in your hand.

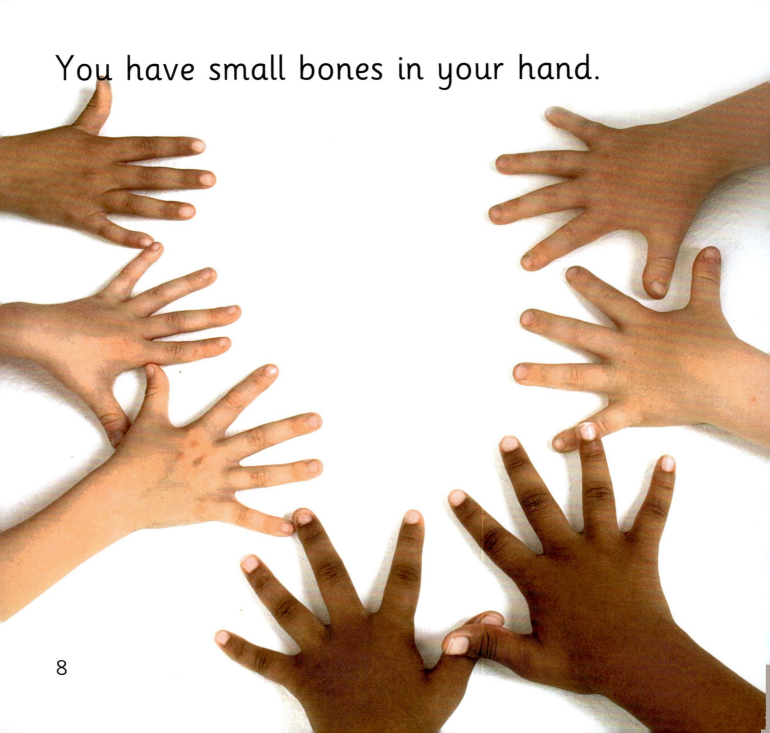

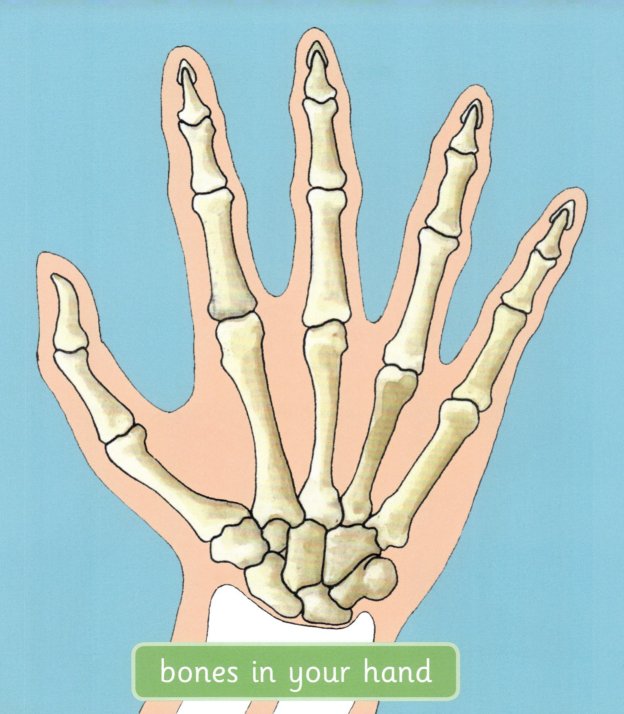

bones in your hand

You have big bones in your legs.

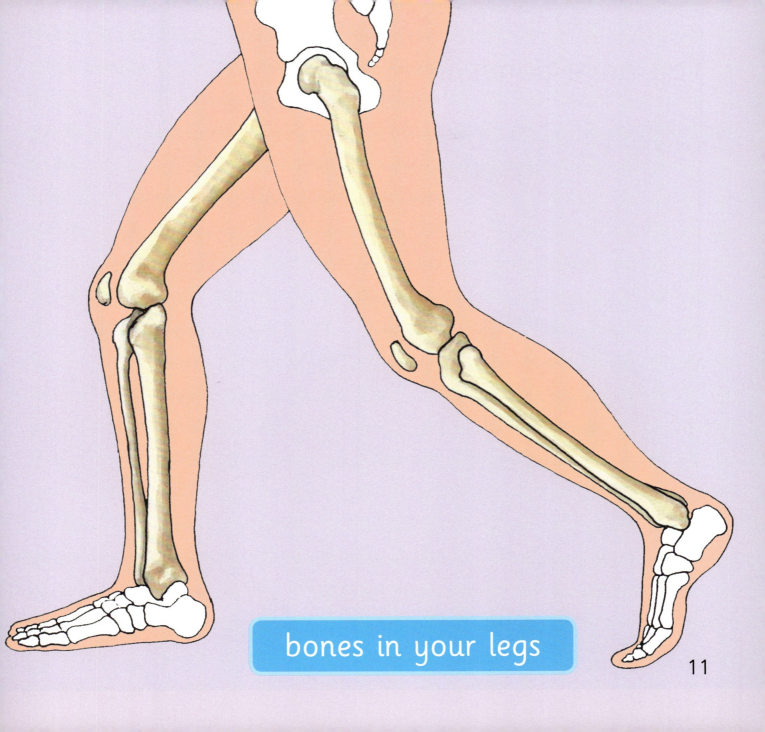

bones in your legs

You have bones in your foot.

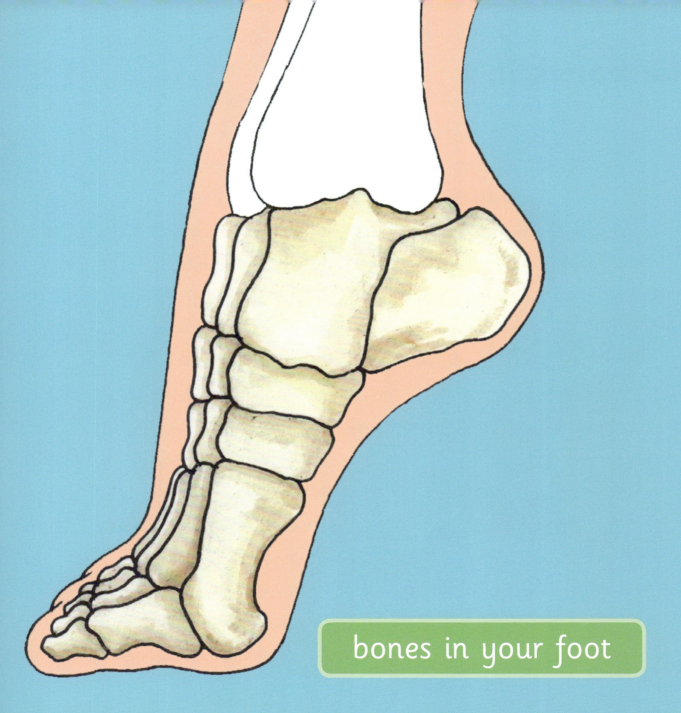

bones in your foot

# The bones in your body

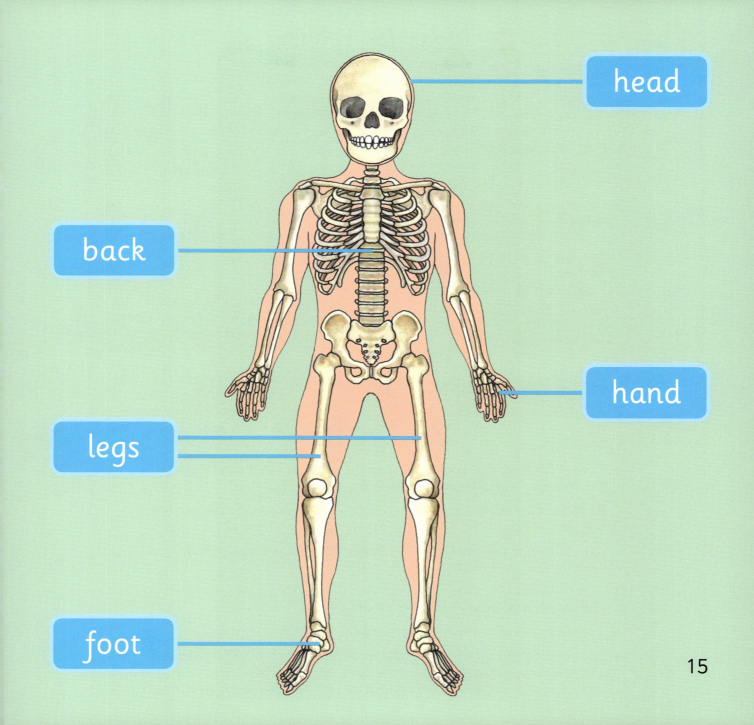

head

back

hand

legs

foot

15

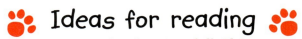# Ideas for reading

Written by Clare Dowdall, PhD
*Lecturer and Primary Literacy Consultant*

**Reading objectives:**
- read and understand simple sentences
- demonstrate understanding when talking with others about what they have read

**Communication and language objectives:**
- express themselves effectively, showing awareness of listeners' needs
- listen attentively in a range of situations
- follow instructions involving several ideas or actions
- give their attention to what others say and respond appropriately

- develop their own narratives and explanations by connecting ideas or events

**Curriculum links:** Knowledge and Understanding of the World

**High frequency words:** you, in

**Interest words:** bones, body, head, back, hand, legs, foot

**Word count:** 67

**Resources:** sticky notes, books and ICT for research, large sheets of paper and marker pens, crayons or chalk

## Build a context for reading

- Ask children to tell each other what they know about their bones. Can they name any of their bones? Which bones are large and which bones are small? What do bones do?

- Look at the front and back covers together. Discuss what can be seen in the pictures. Introduce the word *skeleton*.

- Read the title and blurb aloud with the children, pointing to the words as you read.

- Ask children to feel their hands for bones. How many bones can they feel? Are they large or small?

## Understand and apply reading strategies

- Turn to pp2–3. Ask a volunteer to read the words to the group.

- Look at the picture on p3. Ask children to name any parts of the skeleton that they know. Point to some of the parts, e.g. back, head, legs and introduce this vocabulary. Get children to feel their own back, head and legs.